responsible BUT not perfect

by

Helen Adedamola Agboola

RoseDog Books
PITTSBURGH, PENNSYLVANIA 15238

DEDICATION

To the one who inspires me and calls me "My Albert Einstein", to my daughter who loves me lavishly. My family for their support, friends who believe in my dreams and to my readers who this piece will bring back what they assumed is gone forever. Who will re-create a second chance to bond, make more memories and love again.

Let's soar.

Foreword

The lines of this thirty days nugget are written with sincere desire to help those who struggle to live simpler, nobler and beautiful moments with their partners, spouses, friends, knowing no one is perfect.

Some may wonder why a young woman should advocate for partners who clearly fall often into the category of ones who hurt by their imperfections, carelessness, manly attitudes and ability to take strong decisions. Trust me, it is high time we looked past our partner's flaws, accusing and judging all the time while denying them to experience the feelings that come with some of their good deeds, those moments they displayed heroic roles. The words here are thoughtful, carved out of burning desire to appreciate and celebrate partners, re-untie bonds, re-create or bring back to life a seemingly dead union, knowing fully well that we all aren't perfect.

nugget one

A journey without walking locked in your path would have
been energy drained. A life without crossing you is not a
complete one.

nugget two

Creating plan charts with you is a great based foundation for success. Out of many we created, your attitude to steps to have a working goal is top notch.

nugget THree

This one thing you have done out of many left me astonished.

Your worth can never be underestimated.

nugget four

It's a fresh dew, the nature is calm, the sky is clear, you in my thoughts give a clear vision. It's Ok for you to cloud me.

nugget Five

You have always been a driving force, making each and every

step you take count towards achieving our goals.

nugget six

Our differences give me reasons to love you more.

nugget seven

Have you ever come across a realist? I have one in my world.

You deal with things the way they really are.

NUGGET EIGHT

Observation is key to having an intentional life, you paying attention to details saved us countless times.

nugget nine

In your silence, your actions make life easier. In your darkest mood, your partnership duty never suffers.

nugget ten

You are a blessing but I call you abundance, you live to make

others okay, the win is yours always.

nugget eleven

Disappointment does not stop you.

Failure has no grip on you.

Toxic environment does not impact you negatively.

You walk in your space without distraction.

nugget twelve

The ability to manage your pain to solve other people's troubles is a rare gift. Your attitude towards others' challenges to get them settled amuse me. I call you SOLVER.

nugget Thirteen

Your directional and intentional strength paddles softly and

comfortably, your moves into becoming ever sailing ship

makes me wonder.

nUGGET FOURTEEN

Risk bearer; I have known you to stay at the risk front just to

save your loved ones.

nUggeT FiFteen

In my heart you are ever fresh dew, a drop of you pops me up.

You are calm and powerful.

nugget sixteen

The fatherly role you intensify is another part of you I

never discovered.

nugget seventeen

The sacrifices you make for us, prepare the future we always wanted.

nugget eighteen

Haven thought about you, the way you sort us gives me

more confidence.

nugget nineteen

One with you is more like in the midst of millions of

movable minds.

nugget twenty

Mention a being of many encapsulating thoughts and I will vote

for you a million times.

nugget twenty·one

In nothing, you bring out folds of amazing and

magnificent comfort.

NUGGET TWENTY-TWO

Hmmmm!!! Is there anything you set your mind to do?

Achievement is 100% before you commence.

NUGGET TWENTY-THREE

A trace and legacy is what you leave behind in any direction

you journey.

nugget twenty-four

Show me a deserted space and I will present to you a

dynamic one who will with embedded critical thinking

create a city from it.

nugget twenty·five

A man of his own mind, thoughts and logical reasoning

distinguishes your person from all.

nugget twenty-six

He plans like he is careless yet mindful of every detail about us.

nugget twenty-seven

Man of the people, who does the needful in the face of anger.

Also cares when his actions speak the opposite.

NUGGET TWENTY·EIGHT

Simple yet tough, directional yet fun-loving, playful yet focused,

distracted yet determined.

nugget twenty-nine

Many are seated at his table unknown to them that his own

people are not on the table: you switch when they feel they

know you too well to protect your own people.

nugget thirty

Light of his world…………..happy are you when

everyone is fine.